The World of Plants

Michael L. Macceca

Life Science Readers:
The World of Plants

Publishing Credits

Editorial Director
Dona Herweck Rice

Creative Director
Lee Aucoin

Associate Editor
Joshua BishopRoby

Illustration Manager
Timothy J. Bradley

Editor-in-Chief
Sharon Coan, M.S.Ed.

Publisher
Rachelle Cracchiolo, M.S.Ed.

Science Contributor
Sally Ride Science™

Science Consultants
Thomas R. Ciccone, B.S., M.A. Ed.
 Chino Hills High School
Dr. Ronald Edwards,
 DePaul University

Teacher Created Materials

5301 Oceanus Drive
Huntington Beach, CA 92649-1030
http://www.tcmpub.com
ISBN 978-0-7439-0589-3
© 2008 Teacher Created Materials, Inc.

Table of Contents

All life on Earth needs energy to survive.

Energy is all around us, every day, all the time. We can't escape it. Every living thing on Earth needs energy to survive.

Energy is the force that powers the universe. It makes the stars shine, keeps the planets spinning, warms Earth, and makes plants grow. Energy is very important.

The plants and animals, including people, on Earth get almost all their energy from the sun. Endless amounts of energy stream through space to Earth in the form of heat and light. It is this heat and light energy that plants use to grow. When a plant captures energy, it is stored inside the plant to be used later. Usually it is used to produce more plants by making seeds, flowers, or fruit. Animals take advantage of this **conversion** of energy by harvesting and eating the plants.

Flower Power
Did you know that the bushy part of broccoli is really the flower of the plant? And strawberries grow as part of a flower. Which would you rather eat?

Energy Makes the World Go Round

Energy enters our **environment** and is used in many different ways. When energy is used, it is changed by the work that it does. Earth absorbs the sun's energy. This energy is put to work in many ways. It is the main energy source that powers our environment. Heat from the sun causes water to **evaporate** into the sky. The water **vapor** condenses to form clouds. Rain that falls from the clouds is collected in lakes, rivers, and streams. It is then put to work to make electricity for us. The water also allows plants to grow. This cycle is repeated over and over. It helps make life on Earth possible.

Energy from the sun powers the water cycle, bringing water to plants all over the world.

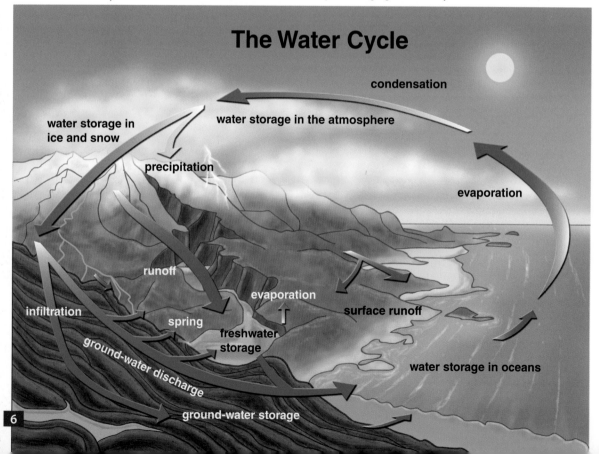

The Water Cycle

condensation

water storage in ice and snow

water storage in the atmosphere

precipitation

evaporation

runoff

evaporation

infiltration

surface runoff

spring

freshwater storage

ground-water discharge

water storage in oceans

ground-water storage

What Is Electricity?

Energy from the sun is used in many ways. One is to make electricity. Hot and cold air cause wind currents. The currents turn wind turbines. Water that falls to the earth is collected behind dams. It is then used to make hydroelectric power. Solar energy panels convert the sun's light energy directly to usable electricity.

Electricity made in one of these ways is called **green energy**. It does not pollute the environment. The energy source is also renewable.

Most electricity today is made by burning fossil fuels, though. Fossil fuels include things such as coal or oil. Electricity can also be made by a nuclear reactor. Electricity made in these ways creates harmful pollution.

Earth's Built-In Power Plant

Some power plants use heat from a volcano. The heat comes from inside the earth. It is used to make electricity. This is called **geothermal energy**.

What Is a Plant?

Plants are living things. They grow in almost every environment on the earth. They grow on the tops of mountains. Some grow in the snow. Some grow in the middle of the desert. No matter where they are, all plants need sun, water, air, and food to grow.

Most things we recognize as plants, such as trees and bushes, have **leaves**, **stems**, and **roots**. Each of these parts does a different task that is needed for the plant to grow. All plants use a process called **photosynthesis** (foh-toh-SIN-thuh-sis) to make their food.

▲ Plants grow in most environments on the earth.

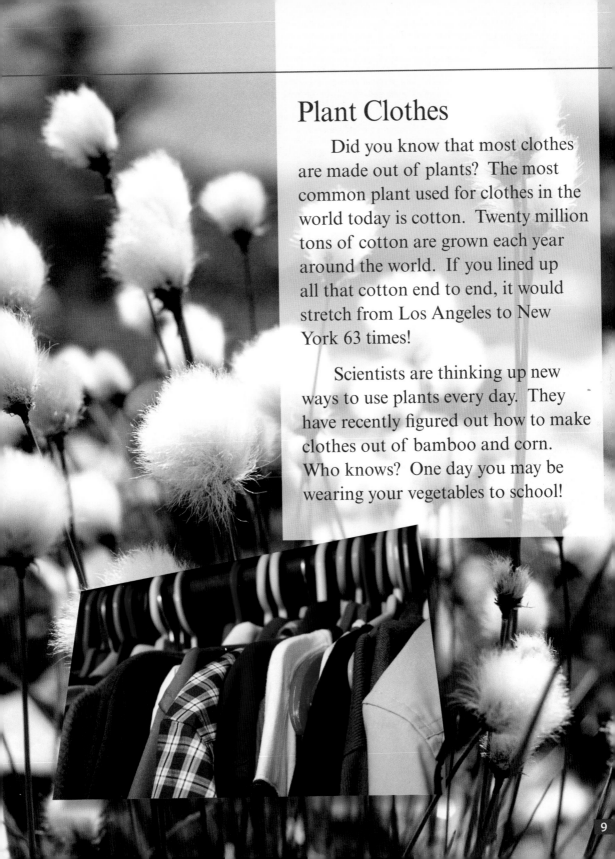

Plant Clothes

Did you know that most clothes are made out of plants? The most common plant used for clothes in the world today is cotton. Twenty million tons of cotton are grown each year around the world. If you lined up all that cotton end to end, it would stretch from Los Angeles to New York 63 times!

Scientists are thinking up new ways to use plants every day. They have recently figured out how to make clothes out of bamboo and corn. Who knows? One day you may be wearing your vegetables to school!

Roots

Plants are anchored to the ground by their roots. This keeps them securely in place during bad weather or when an animal rubs against them. But roots do a lot more than keep a plant in place. The roots' most important role is taking in **nutrients** from the **soil**. The roots branch out into the soil to get water. The water has nutrients from the soil dissolved in it. Some of these nutrients come from plants that have died and are now rotting.

When a plant dies, it **decomposes**. All the nutrients that are stored in it return to the soil. More nutrients come from decomposing animals and microorganisms. New plants use these nutrients to grow. Lawns and gardens need these same nutrients. Since we don't often keep decomposing plants in our yards, we have to add **fertilizer** (FUR-tuhl-eye-zer). Fertilizer has all the nutrients that plants need.

You can see the decomposing bits of plant stalks and leaves in this handful of soil.

Roots reach down into the soil. They gather water and nutrients and also keep the plant from washing or blowing away.

Unusual Roots

The banyan tree has roots that grow down from the branches to the ground. The roots help support the branches of the trees. The trees can grow big enough to shade a whole village.

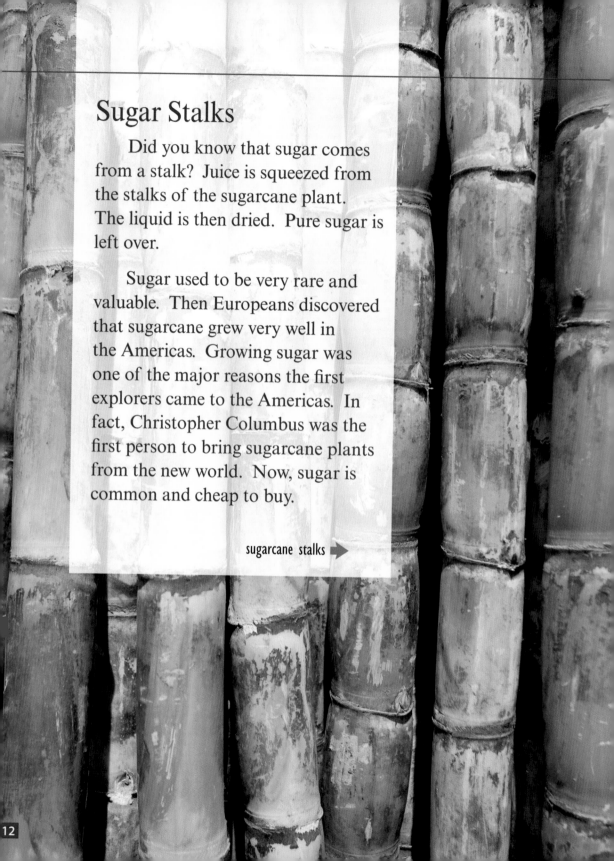

Sugar Stalks

Did you know that sugar comes from a stalk? Juice is squeezed from the stalks of the sugarcane plant. The liquid is then dried. Pure sugar is left over.

Sugar used to be very rare and valuable. Then Europeans discovered that sugarcane grew very well in the Americas. Growing sugar was one of the major reasons the first explorers came to the Americas. In fact, Christopher Columbus was the first person to bring sugarcane plants from the new world. Now, sugar is common and cheap to buy.

sugarcane stalks ➡

Stems and Stalks

Stems and stalks hold up plants and give them shape. They also hold the plumbing system of the plant. Water and nutrients are sucked out of the soil by the roots. Then they are sent up to the leaves through tiny pipes, called **xylem** (ZY-luhm). Some water is lost through tiny pores in the stem and leaves called **stomata** (stoh-MAH-tuh). As the plant matures, or grows older, the stems grow longer and bigger around.

Over time, the outside of the stem becomes rough and thick, like **bark**. This helps to protect the plant. Many plants can grow spikes or thorns. These help keep the plants from being eaten by animals.

Inside a Stem

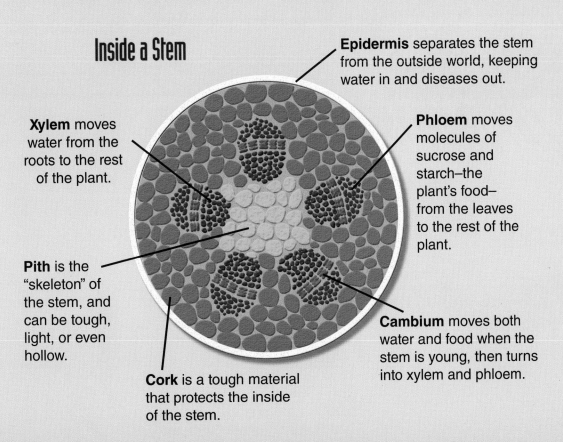

Epidermis separates the stem from the outside world, keeping water in and diseases out.

Xylem moves water from the roots to the rest of the plant.

Phloem moves molecules of sucrose and starch—the plant's food—from the leaves to the rest of the plant.

Pith is the "skeleton" of the stem, and can be tough, light, or even hollow.

Cambium moves both water and food when the stem is young, then turns into xylem and phloem.

Cork is a tough material that protects the inside of the stem.

Leaves

Leaves are the most obvious part of plants and trees. They provide shade for us on hot days. Leaves are pleasant to look at. They also have an important job. Inside the leaves is where all the business of making food for the plant takes place.

Leaves can be found in many shapes and sizes.

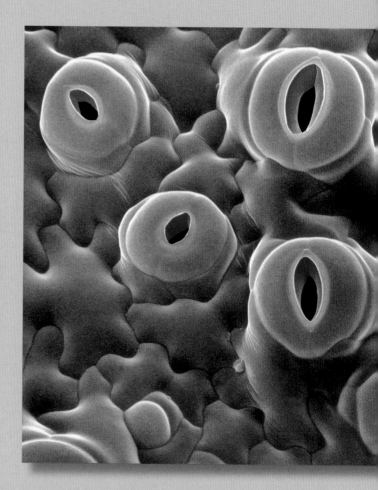

Leaves take on different shapes and sizes. This depends on the weather where they are found. The leaves have adapted to the climate over time. Leaves on pine trees are called needles. Leaves on palm trees are called fronds. Some leaves are soft and hairy, while some are smooth and shiny.

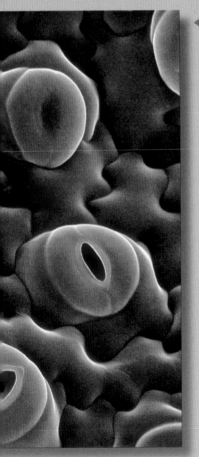

This magnified image shows open stomata on the surface of a leaf. Stomata are pores found on the leaf surface. They control the exchange of gases from the leaf to the atmosphere.

Medicine From Plants? Imagine That.

For thousands of years, people have used natural medicines that they get from plants. This type of medicine is called **herbology.** Leaves, stems, and roots from specially selected plants and trees are used. Then they are blended to target a specific illness. The mixture of herbs or leaves is often brewed into a tea. Then a patient drinks it. People of many cultures have used plants as natural remedies. They've been doing this since before history was recorded. Many modern medicines originated as herbal cures, too. Next time your doctor gives you some medicine, ask her if it came from an herbal cure.

Growth

Plants use the food they make in their leaves. It helps them grow. Why do plants keep growing? Why don't they just grow to a certain size and stop? It is because plants "want" to reproduce. Trees keep growing taller to get more sunshine to make more food. Then, they can make more seeds for new trees. Plants grow wider with bigger leaves for the same reason. Humans have taken advantage of this by **adapting** some plants and trees into crops. The crops produce food for us to eat.

The Redwoods

Redwood trees are the tallest trees in the world and can grow to over 300 feet tall.

Reproduction is a natural part of a plant's life. That is why, in a forest such as this, you will find many of the same kinds of plants and trees.

Trees: A Renewable Resource?

A **resource** is something that we use from nature. A **renewable resource** is able to **regenerate** or be replanted as fast as it is used. For example, corn is used for many different products. We eat it and we feed it to farm animals. We get sweetener and cooking oil from it. We also convert it into fuel and cloth. Farmers plant enough of it every year to meet our needs.

Trees are cut down for use as lumber. The lumber makes up the skeletons of many houses and buildings. Until recently, trees were thought to be an endless renewable resource. Whole mountains were stripped of all their trees. This was done by a practice called **clear-cutting**. Then people realized the trees couldn't grow back without our help. Now, the lumber industry practices **selective cutting**. Only some trees are removed from the forest. This leaves a lot of trees to help repopulate the forest.

Rings of Age

You can tell how old a tree is by counting its growth rings. The oldest living things on the earth are the bristlecone pine trees in California. The oldest tree there is named Methuselah. It is nearly 4,800 years old!

Pests: Hey, Quit Bugging Me

Have you ever bitten into an apple and found a worm? The worm is considered a **pest**. People grow plants to eat the food they produce. There are always other living things that want to eat the plants, too. We can build a fence to keep some animals away. That doesn't work for smaller pests like worms and bugs.

The smaller pests can be anything that wants our food. They can be wasps or worms. But there are very small organisms we can't see, called **microbes**. They can cause diseases in the plants. Farmers use chemicals called **pesticides**. These are **toxic** to the pests. The chemicals are sometimes

injected as a gas directly into the soil. Or they are sprayed on the crops from an airplane.

Organic farms are different. They do not use pesticides. Organic farmers believe this makes their food safer to eat. But the food is more expensive because the pests eat their share.

Pesticides can be sprayed onto crops with an airplane called a crop duster.

Ant Farm

The leafcutting ants in Central America grow their own crops. They bring leaf cuttings to their nests. Then they feed the cuttings to their "fungus gardens." The ants harvest the fungus for food.

Photosynthesis

Plants keep growing their entire lives. They never stop. Some grow slowly and some grow fast. Where do they get the energy to keep growing? They get it from the food that they make for themselves.

Leaves are made up of tiny parts called **cells**. Leaves are green because of a substance called **chlorophyll** (KLOR-uh-fil) in the cells. These little green molecules are like tiny factories. They use sunlight to turn air and water into food for the plant. This process is called photosynthesis. Without photosynthesis, life would not be possible on Earth. Plants use **carbon dioxide** gas from the air to make food. Then they release **oxygen** as a byproduct.

upper surface of the leaf

vertical cells containing chlorophyll

vascular tubes

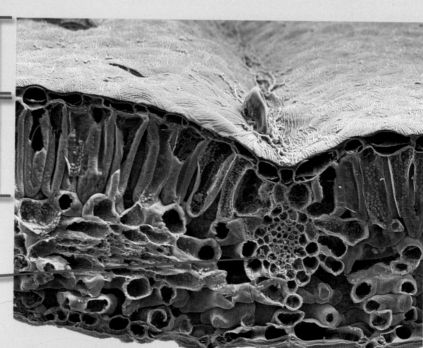

▲ Using a powerful microscope to look at a leaf, you can see the cells containing green chlorophyll. In the middle of this picture, you can also see a bundle of vascular tubes. The food made in the leaf goes through the tubes to the rest of the plant.

Every living thing needs to breathe oxygen to live. Dogs and cats, bugs and people, and even plants need oxygen.

Get Off My Back

A saprophyte (SAP-ruh-fite) is a plant that does not photosynthesize. Sometimes it steals its food from other plants. It can also be called a parasite.

Respiration

Photosynthesis takes in carbon dioxide and releases oxygen. This is a good thing for us. Animals need to breathe in oxygen to turn food into energy. We then breathe out carbon dioxide. Using oxygen to turn food into energy is called **respiration**. Plants respire, too. But they only use a little of the oxygen that they produce. That means there's some left over for us!

The Motion in the Ocean

If you were to go swimming in the ocean, you would probably see some fish. You would also see many different kinds of organisms. One kind of seaweed, called kelp, grows close to the shore. It is green and leafy. You might think it is a plant, but it is a kind of organism called an **algae**. Other algae are so small you can hardly see them. Algae and seaweed photosynthesize just like plants on land do.

They certainly don't have any trouble finding water. It's all around them. When algae make food, they release oxygen into the water. Fish use some of the oxygen to breathe. Some of the oxygen is released into the air. Since the earth is mostly covered with oceans, many scientists believe algae are the most important source of oxygen on the planet.

Plant or Animal?

Coral is not a plant. It is a whole colony of very small animals. The animals are called polyps. They live inside the protective shells we call coral.

You Eat Seaweed!

That's right. Seaweed is used in many different things we eat. It is used to thicken things up or make them gooey. Toothpaste, yogurt, and your favorite candies all have seaweed in them. The most common use of seaweed is ice cream.

↑ seaweed

The World of Plants

Plants are found in almost every kind of environment on the earth. There are plants that survive in the snow near the North Pole. There are plants that live in the hottest desert. Wherever they are found, plants are prepared for their environment. For instance, palm trees are tall and have a flexible trunk. When a tropical storm blows through, the palm tree bobs back and forth, but it doesn't break.

Palm trees did not become flexible so that they could survive storms. It took millions of years for the palm tree to develop. Each new tree was a little different from the tree before it. Some of the trees weren't flexible. They broke under the high winds. The trees that were flexible survived. Their seeds became the next trees, which were also flexible. Eventually, they became the palm trees we know today.

Plants are found all over the world, in all different shapes and colors.

Orchids Live on Air?

Air plants are plants that do not require any soil. They absorb all of their water and nutrients from the air. Most orchids are air plants.

The pinyon pine has single needles that are very short because it lives where the climate is cold and dry.

All Leaves Are Not Created Equal

Have you noticed that each type of tree has leaves of a different shape and size? Leaves are the part of a plant that is most exposed to its environment. For this reason, you can see how a plant or tree has adapted to its environment by looking at its leaves.

Cactus leaves are actually its spines. They have adapted to the high heat and sun exposure of the desert.

Pine needles are also a modified version of leaves. These photos show how the length of the needle and the number per bundle varies, depending on the weather where a pine grows.

The ponderosa pine has bundles of three long needles and lives where there is plenty of water and warm summers.

Plants are a vital part of our world. Animals breathe the oxygen that plants make and release carbon dioxide that plants use. During photosynthesis, plants produce food to help them grow. Animals eat plants to benefit from this food also.

Plants have adapted over millions of years to live in almost every environment on the earth. People have also adapted some plants for use as food. Farmers grow crops in very large amounts so they can supply whole cities of people with food.

Next time you relax under a tree, remember there is a lot of work going on inside that tree. The roots are taking in water and nutrients. The water and nutrients are carried to the leaves and made into food for the tree. The tree makes more leaves, and maybe nuts or fruits, as it continues to grow toward the sky.

The Venus flytrap gets some of its nutrients from insects it catches in its "mouth."

▲ We benefit from plants every day, whether it's
the food we eat or a shady spot under a tree.

: Transportation Within Plants

We can't see plants grow because they grow so slowly. We do know that plants drink water and nutrients from the earth. Otherwise, they would wilt and die.

To learn more about plants, do an experiment to prove that water is transported from the roots, up the stalk, and out to the leaves of a plant.

Materials

- beaker
- water
- red food coloring
- stalk of celery

Procedure

1 Fill a large glass or beaker with water and add red food coloring until it is dark red.

2 Place the stalk of celery into the beaker and allow it to sit for a while.

3 After some time, the red water will flow through the plant and turn the tips of the leaves red.

4 Peel off one stalk and slice it in half. You will see the small tubes that carry water and nutrients to the leaves.

Conclusion

1 Describe what you observe in the celery. Why do you think you see what you see?

2 What do you think would happen if you turned the stalk upside down and placed the leaves in the colored water? Why?

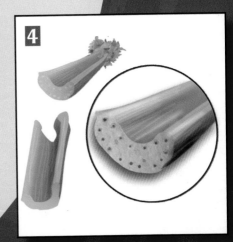

Glossary

adapting—changing

algae—microscopic plants that live in the ocean

bark—the protective coating of a plant or tree

carbon dioxide—a gas that is converted to oxygen through photosynthesis

cells—the individual units that make up all living things

chlorophyll—green substance found in plant cells that allows photosynthesis to occur

clear-cutting—a management technique in which all the trees in an area are cut down at the same time

conversion—when something is changed from one thing to another

decompose—to break something down into its individual parts

energy—the power needed to do work

environment—our surroundings

evaporate—when a liquid dries up and converts into a gas

fertilizer—nutrients that are added to soil from decomposing plants or animals

geothermal—heat from volcanic activity inside the earth

green energy—energy made from renewable sources

herbology—the ancient practice of using plants for medicine

leaves—the green part of the plant where photosynthesis occurs

microbe—a very small organism that is usually harmful to plants

nutrients—the building blocks that plants use to make food

organic—from natural sources; without pesticides

oxygen—a gas that is a byproduct of photosynthesis that we need to breathe

pest—an undesirable organism that is harmful to plants

pesticide—something that is used to kill pests

photosynthesis—the process of making food from light energy

regenerate—to reproduce or renew something that is lost

renewable resource—materials, such as plants and trees, that are able to regenerate and won't run out

resource—something supplied by nature

respiration—breathing; exchanging one gas for another

root—the underground part of the plant that takes up water and nutrients

selective cutting—the periodic removal of individual trees or groups of trees

soil—nutrient-rich earth that is suitable for plants to grow in

stem—the tall, rigid part of a plant that is responsible for its height

stomata—tiny pores in a plant

toxic—harmful, especially by chemical means; poisonous

vapor—the gas form of a liquid

xylem—tiny tubes in a plant that carry water up from its roots to the rest of the plant

Index

Sally Ride Science™ is an innovative content company dedicated to fueling young people's interests in science. Our publications and programs provide opportunities for students and teachers to explore the captivating world of science—from astrobiology to zoology. We bring science to life and show young people that science is creative, collaborative, fascinating, and fun.

Image Credits